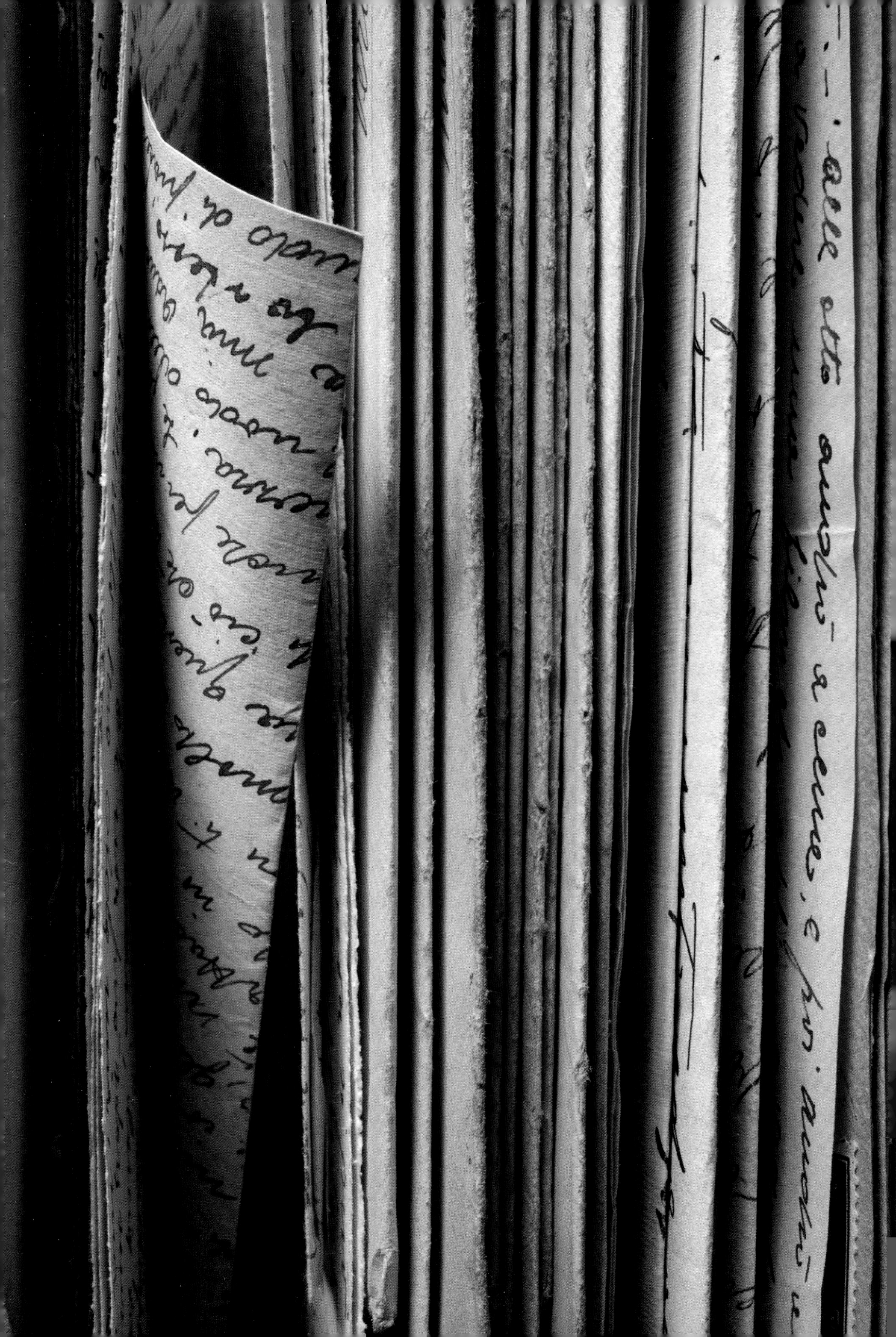

Organized Essays

Valerie Bodden

CREATIVE EDUCATION

Published by Creative Education

P.O. Box 227, Mankato, Minnesota 56002

Creative Education is an imprint of The Creative Company

www.thecreativecompany.us

Design and art direction by Rita Marshall

Production by The Design Lab

Printed by Corporate Graphics in the United States of America

Photographs by Alamy (Mary Evans Picture Library), Corbis (Bettmann, Christopher Felver, Historical Picture Archive, Stacy Morrison), Dreamstime (Pindiyath100), Getty Images (Jeffrey Coolidge, After Paul van Somer, Hank Walker/Time & Life Pictures), iStockphoto (Don Bayley, Trevor Hunt, Aldo Ottaviani)

Excerpt on page 26 from "Grant and Lee: A Study in Contrasts" by Bruce Catton. Copyright U.S. Capitol Historical Society, all rights reserved. Reprinted by permission.

Excerpt on page 38 from "The Way to Rainy Mountain" from *The Way to Rainy Mountain* by N. Scott Momaday. Copyright © 1969 by the University of New Mexico Press. Reprinted by permission.

Library of Congress Cataloging-in-Publication Data

Bodden, Valerie.

Organized essays / by Valerie Bodden.

p. cm. — (Nonfiction: writing for fact and argument)

Includes bibliographical references and index.

Summary: An introduction to the ways that writers compose well-structured essays. Excerpts and analysis help to explain the importance of perspective and research in this nonfiction form.

ISBN 978-1-58341-933-5

1. Essay—Authorship—Juvenile literature. I. Title.

PN4500.B63 2010   808.4—dc22   2009024045

CPSIA: 120109 PO1094

First Edition

9 8 7 6 5 4 3 2 1

ONTENTS

Maybe your heart thumps with excitement at the thought of a new adventure novel. Perhaps you get goosebumps as you delve into mystery stories. But what if someone hands you an essay to read? Do you yawn? Set it aside? Say "no thank you"? `Nonfiction` *works such as essays don't always spark the same enthusiasm as works of* `fiction` *, but nonfiction can be as entertaining, engaging, and exciting as fiction. In fact, sometimes it is more so, offering us insight about life as only the real world can. The best nonfiction writing has the power to teach or persuade, enrage or enliven, sadden or surprise.*

Of all nonfiction forms, the essay is perhaps the most flexible. It can be short or long (although most essays are shorter than book-length). It can be formal or informal, personal or impersonal, funny or tragic. And it can cover just about any topic, from weighty issues such as war and death to lighthearted subjects such as circuses and Sunday afternoons. One well-known author has even written an essay about potato chips.

Just because the essay is a flexible form, however, does not necessarily mean that essays are easy to write. Essays need to be organized so that readers can follow them. They need to be compelling so that potential readers will be motivated to pick them up. And, above all, essays must make a point. If the essay is successful, that point will stick with readers long after they have read the last word.

The roots of the essay can be found in ancient Greece and Rome, where writers such as Plato, Seneca, and Plutarch penned letters, `dialogues`, and other works that, although usually not considered essays in themselves, would influence later essay writers. Most notably, their works inspired Michel de Montaigne, a 16th-century Frenchman whom most scholars consider to be the first true essayist. Montaigne called his pieces *essais*, which means "attempts" or "trials" in French.

By the late 16th century, an English writer named Francis Bacon had begun to write his own essays. Although Bacon adopted the same term as Montaigne had for his writing, his pieces were quite different from those of the Frenchman. While both authors often wrote about philosophy and human nature, Montaigne's essays tended to be informal and intimate and openly revealed something about himself (for example, that he was short and loud). Bacon's works, on the other hand, were generally formal and impersonal, with little trace of the author or his personality to be found in them.

During the 17th century, essay writing was taken up by several authors in England, most of whom wrote

about solemn topics such as death and melancholy.
Essays did not become truly popular, however, until
the 18th century, with the development of periodicals—regularly published newspapers and magazines.
Periodicals gave essayists a reliable means of
distributing their works, which had before been
published in occasional pamphlets. Among the first
periodicals to feature essays were *The Tatler* and
The Spectator, published collaboratively in England

Writer Francis Bacon
(1561–1626)

by Richard Steele and Joseph Addison. In the pages of these periodicals, Steele and Addison offered lighthearted, often amusing essays that nevertheless usually managed to impart a moral or lesson to readers. The following excerpt is taken from Addison's essay "A Lady's Head-Dress," published in *The Spectator* in 1711. As you read the essay, notice how Addison gently makes fun of the changing styles of ladies' hair pieces. What point do you think he is trying to make?

The inaugural 1709 issue of *The Tatler*

There is not so variable a thing in nature as a lady's head-dress. Within my own memory I have known it rise and fall above thirty degrees. About ten years ago it shot up to a very great height, insomuch that the female part of our species were much taller than the men. The women were of such an enormous stature, that "we appeared as grasshoppers before them"; at present the whole sex is in a manner dwarfed, and shrunk into a race of beauties that seems almost another species. I remember several ladies, who were once very near seven foot high, that at present want some inches of five.... I find most are of opinion [that] they are at present like trees new lopped and pruned, that will certainly sprout up and flourish with greater heads than before. For my own part, as I do not love to be insulted by women who are taller than myself, I admire the sex much more in their present humiliation, which has reduced them to their natural dimensions, than when they had extended their persons and lengthened themselves out into formidable and gigantic figures....

I would desire the fair sex to consider how impossible it is for them to add anything that can be ornamental to what is already the masterpiece of nature. The head has the most beautiful appearance, as well as the highest station, in a human figure. Nature has laid out all her art in beautifying the face; ... and surrounded it with such a flowing shade of hair as sets all its beauties in the most agreeable light.... When we load [the head] with such a pile of ... ornaments, we ... foolishly contrive to call off the eye from great and real beauties, to childish gewgaws [trinkets], ribands [ribbons], and bonelace.

As you read this essay, you could probably picture women with their heads piled high in lace and ribbons. Perhaps it even made you laugh to think what women used to do to their hair in an attempt at beauty. But Addison's essay isn't intended only to make fun of his female readership; it also pays compliment to women and points out the folly of seeking beauty through material ornamentation.

Throughout the remainder of the 18th century, other periodicals tried to reproduce the light-hearted feel of the essays in Addison and Steele's newspapers, but most did not succeed. By the beginning of the 19th century, however, new essayists such as Englishmen Charles Lamb and William Hazlitt rose to prominence, making the form more personal by writing about their own adventures and insights. It wasn't long, though, before the Victorian Age brought with it a return of the formal essay, with a focus on largely serious, academic topics such as history and literature. At the same time, the essay was finally beginning to be developed in the United States through writers such as Ralph Waldo Emerson and Henry David

An exaggerated illustration of a British woman in a headdress

Thoreau. In China, Japan, Russia, Germany, and elsewhere throughout Europe and Asia, essays were also increasing in prominence.

By the beginning of the 20th century, essayists were again pushing toward a more personal, informal style, with pieces that examined their innermost thoughts and motives. After World War I (1914–18), essay writers began to focus on current—and often controversial—events such as war and politics, using the form to boldly express their opinions. The essay thrived throughout the 1950s, especially in the U.S., where writers such as Mary McCarthy, Edmund Wilson, and James Baldwin made names for themselves. Essays were discussed not only by the "literary" upper class but also by working-class citizens such as factory workers and farmers. Views on the role of the essay in today's world vary; some scholars believe the essay has largely been replaced by other literary forms, while others insist that essays, and especially personal essays, are more popular today than ever before. So pick up a periodical or a book of essays and see for yourself why the form has endured for more than 500 years!

Forms and Functions

When you think of an essay, what probably comes to mind is the formal essay. Formal essays are generally written about a specific topic for a specific purpose—usually to inform or persuade the reader. The topic you choose doesn't always determine whether your essay will inform or persuade, though. For example, an essay about cattle ranching could be informative, focusing on the lifestyle of cattle ranchers. Or, it could be persuasive, arguing, for instance, that cattle ranching harms the environment. The difference is that in the first essay, you are simply trying to teach your readers something interesting that they didn't know before; in the second, you are trying to convince them that your point of view is the right one, and you may even attempt to lead them to take action of some sort.

Of all formal essays, probably none is more formal than the research paper. Research papers are not simply a presentation of your own ideas (no matter how well thought out). As the name implies, a research paper is based on research. In it, you set forth an idea, or thesis, that you then prove with the support of reliable sources, which you carefully document. In general, the thesis of a research paper offers an opinion or interpretation, though it does not have to be controversial. For example, you could set out to prove that the character of Professor Severus Snape in J. K. Rowling's *Harry Potter* books is a `tragic hero`. In order to do so, you would provide proof both from Rowling's books and from others who have researched and written about the topic.

Unlike formal essays such as research papers, personal essays rely not on outside sources but on what you think and have experienced. Because of this, many new writers believe that personal essays must be easy to write. After all, what could be easier than simply transferring thoughts from your brain to the page? Personal essays aren't a random collection of thoughts or even of personal stories, though. Like all good essays, they need to make a point. Although your personal essay is about something that has happened to you, it should also include a grain of truth or universal message that readers can apply to their own lives. They might not have had the same experience you had, but likely they've had the same feelings and can identify with you in some way.

The following excerpt from the essay "A Relic" (1918) by English writer Max Beerbohm tells of the memories the discovery of an old, broken fan calls up in the author. As you read, pay attention to why this item is important to the writer. Can you identify with his experience in any way?

A cartoon illustration of author
Max Beerbohm (1872-1956)

[The pieces of the fan have] no market value.... And yet, though I had so long forgotten them, for me they are not worthless. They touch a chord.... Lest this confession raise false hopes in the reader, I add that I did not know their owner.

I did once see her.... She was graceful, she was even beautiful. I was but nineteen years old.... I was seated at a table of a café on the terrace of a casino.... I heard the swing-door behind me flap open, and was aware of a sharp snapping and crackling sound as a lady in white passed quickly by me.... A short, fat man passed in pursuit of her.... I saw that she had left a trail of little white things on the asphalt.... What was the matter? What had made her so spectacularly angry with him?... [The waiter] stooped down and picked up something which, with a smile and a shrug he laid on my table.... This is the thing I now write of....

I was not destined to see either [the man or the woman] again....

They made, however, a prolonged stay in my young memory, and would have done so even had I not had that tangible memento of them.... Again and again I would take the fan-stump from my pocket, examining it on the palm of my hand, or between finger and thumb, hoping to read the mystery it had been mixed up in, so that I might reveal that mystery to the world.... I was determined to make a story of what I had seen....

The chord this relic strikes in me is not one of curiosity as to that old quarrel, but (if you will forgive me) one of tenderness for my first effort to write, and for my first hopes of excellence.

There, in the last line, we are brought into
the point of Beerbohm's whole essay. It's what
makes this more than simply an anecdote, or brief
story. Beerbohm shows us that the fan has value
not because of what it is or who it belonged to or
how he obtained it but because of the change it
brought about in him. It led him to pick up a pen
and make his first attempt at writing. Although
most of us probably have not received a broken fan

discarded by a fighting couple, we can still relate
to this story. We, too, have experienced moments
that have changed our lives. And, like Beerbohm,
we cherish items not because of what they are but
because of the memories they hold. Maybe you keep
an old baseball glove simply because it was the one
you were wearing when you came to love the game,
for example. Beerbohm has given us insight into
not only his experience but also our own.

Along with helping readers see something in
their lives more clearly, writing personal essays
can help writers deal with issues in their own
lives. Authors often write about difficult or
painful experiences in order to help themselves
sort through their emotions and come to a better
understanding of how those experiences have shaped
them. So don't be afraid to examine your life on
the page. Who knows what you—and your readers—
might learn!

Before you can write an essay of any kind, you obviously must decide what to write about. Although your topic can be nearly any person, place, or thing, you should not try to write about that person, place, or thing as a whole. If you do so, you will not only assign yourself an impossible task, but you will also end up with an essay that lacks a clear organizing focus. You need to narrow your idea to a specific topic. If you want to write about television, for example, you might examine the effect of television's development on radio or the amount of television children watch each day or why you prefer one television show over another. Of course, which topic you choose will probably depend at least in part on what type of essay you are writing. A topic for a research paper, for example, must be one that you can examine through research (and likely very little has been written by others about your personal television preferences).

If your essay does happen to be a research paper, your next step will be to research the topic. You want to find information to back up your claims. As you research, you will probably rely on a combination of primary sources, such as interviews and scientific studies, and `secondary sources`, such as books and magazine articles. Be sure to take notes as you research. They will help to ensure that your information is accurate, and, if you are writing a research paper, you will need to `cite` the sources of the information you provide.

When you are ready to begin writing, you cannot simply throw all of your facts and thoughts together on the page and expect the result to be a readable essay. You must instead present your ideas in an orderly fashion, so that your reader doesn't get lost in the chaos. Most formal essays begin with an introduction that presents the main idea, followed by a few or dozens of paragraphs to support that idea and a conclusion that brings the piece to a satisfying close. Although personal essays don't necessarily follow the pattern of introduction, body, conclusion, they do have a clear beginning, middle, and end that readers can follow.

Many essays, especially formal ones, introduce a thesis in the introduction. The thesis presents the author's main idea and tells readers what he or she is going to prove in the essay. Some experienced writers choose not to spell out their

thesis. This does not mean that their essay has no thesis, but rather that the thesis is implied instead of stated explicitly . Because personal essays generally deal with an experience rather than an idea, they may have a theme rather than a specific thesis, but they still leave the reader with one main thought.

The following excerpt from American author Bruce Catton's essay "Grant and Lee: A Study in Contrasts" (1956) has an explicit thesis. Try to identify it as you read.

Author Bruce Catton (1899–1978) with miniature Civil War models

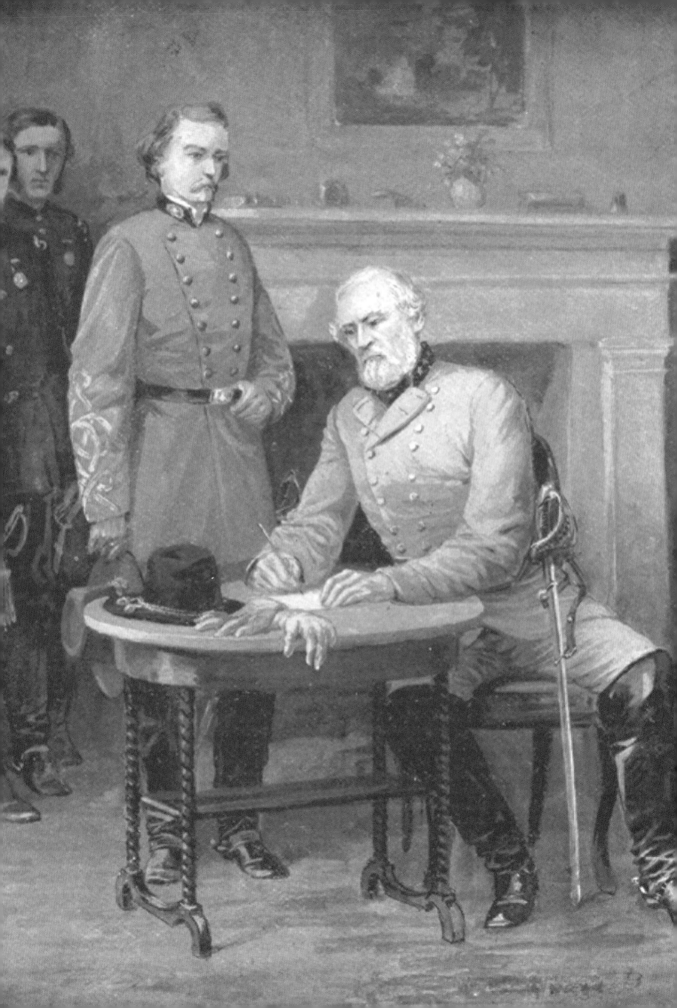

When Ulysses S. Grant and Robert E. Lee met in the parlor of a modest house at Appomattox Court House, Virginia, on April 9, 1865, to work out the terms for the surrender of Lee's Army of Northern Virginia, a great chapter in American life came to a close, and a great new chapter began....

They were two strong men, these oddly different generals, and they represented the strengths of two conflicting currents that, through them, had come into final collision....

Lee was tidewater Virginia, and in his background were family, culture, and tradition.... He embodied a way of life that had come down through the age of knighthood and the English country squire.... Lee stood for the feeling that it was somehow of advantage to human society to have a pronounced inequality in the social structure....

Grant, the son of a tanner on the Western frontier, was everything Lee was not. He had come up the hard way and embodied nothing in particular except the eternal toughness and sinewy fiber of the men who grew up beyond the mountains. He was one of a body of men who ... were self-reliant to a fault, who cared hardly anything for the past but who had a sharp eye for the future....

Different as they were ... these two great soldiers had much in common....

Perhaps greatest of all, there was the ability, at the end, to turn quickly from war to peace once the fighting was over. Out of the way these two men behaved at Appomattox came the possibility of a peace of reconciliation.... Two great Americans, Grant and Lee—very different, yet under everything very much alike. Their encounter at Appomattox was one of the great moments of American history.

Did you catch the thesis of this essay? Catton tells us, "They were two strong men, these oddly different generals, and they represented the strengths of two conflicting currents that, through them, had come into final collision." Then, he goes on to prove his point, showing us exactly how Grant and Lee were different. Notice that not only does Catton's entire essay have a point, but each paragraph does, too. The point is stated in the first sentence of each paragraph, which is usually referred to as the topic sentence (since it sets out the topic of the paragraph). For example, the first sentence of the paragraph about Grant tells us that he "was everything Lee was not." The rest of the paragraph develops the point, showing us exactly how Grant differs from Lee.

Catton piques our curiosity with an introduction that pulls us into the end of the Civil War and the beginning of a "new chapter." His conclusion takes us back to the introduction, reminding us of how important the meeting of these two contrasting generals at Appomattox was to American history. Catton has proved his

thesis and leaves us feeling satisfied that we have understood it. So pick through your facts, line them up, and pull us into them—once you do, we're sure to see your point!

General Robert E. Lee in
Appomattox Court House

Proving a point is not always as easy as it may sound. You cannot simply say, "Here is my point. Here is my proof." First, you must decide *how* you will prove your point. Will you offer definitions and descriptions? Examples and illustrations? Narration? Depending on your topic, you may use any one—or even all—of these techniques, along with several others.

If you want to tell a story, you will use the technique of narration. Many essayists begin their pieces with a short narrative that helps draw the reader in and compels him or her to read on. Personal essays often rely largely on narrative. Max Beerbohm's personal essay on page 18, for example, provides a narrative of how he came to own the broken fan. Many essays that make use of narrative also incorporate a related technique: description. Descriptions based on the five senses help readers picture exactly what you are writing about and add interest to your writing. So if your essay is about water pollution, for example, don't be afraid to include a description of the way a river smells after raw sewage has been emptied into it, if that helps make your point.

In order to add clarity to their writing, essay writers often define key terms. This way, readers know exactly what the writer means when he or she uses a specific word. Definitions don't always rely on dictionaries. In many cases, essayists provide their own vision of what an `abstract` idea—such as love—means. Often, definitions and explanations can be made clearer through the use of examples, or specific illustrations of a general concept. If you are writing about love, for example, you might help readers understand your view if you provide an example of an action you thought demonstrated love—maybe the time your parents threw you a surprise birthday party.

You can also help readers understand more about one subject by comparing or contrasting it with another. Bruce Catton's essay about Generals Grant and Lee on page 25 makes extensive use of this technique. Or, you can divide a subject into smaller parts in order to explain each part more fully. American essayist Russell Baker once wrote an essay in which he divided inanimate objects into three groups: "those that that don't work, those that break down, and those that get lost."

Another way to help readers understand your point is to analyze a process, or tell how something works. Or your essay can examine cause and effect, attempting to explain why something happened or to describe the consequences of some event. And, if the goal of your essay is to do more than teach your readers—if you want to persuade them that you are right—you will need to develop logical arguments, and you may also choose to appeal to their emotions.

As you read the following excerpt from American author Mark Twain's essay "How to Tell a Story" (1895), try to identify the various techniques he uses to make his point.

Author and humorist
Mark Twain (1835–1910)

There are several kinds of stories, but only one difficult kind—the humorous. I will talk mainly about that one. The humorous story is American, the comic story is English, the witty story is French. The humorous story depends for its effect upon the manner *of the telling; the comic story and the witty story upon the* matter.

The humorous story may be spun out to great length, and may wander around as much as it pleases, and arrive nowhere in particular; but the comic and witty stories must be brief and end with a point....

The humorous story is told gravely; the teller does his best to conceal the fact that he even dimly suspects that there is anything funny about it; but the teller of the comic story tells you beforehand that it is one of the funniest things he has ever heard, then tells it with eager delight, and is the first person to laugh when he gets through. And sometimes ... he will repeat the "nub" of it....

Very often, of course, the rambling and disjointed humorous story finishes with a nub, point, snapper, or whatever you like to call it. Then the listener must be alert, for in many cases the teller will divert attention from that nub by dropping it in a carefully casual and indifferent way, with the pretense that he does not know it is a nub.

[American humorist] Artemus Ward used that trick a good deal; then when the belated audience presently caught the joke he would look up with innocent surprise, as if wondering what they had found to laugh at....

Let me set down an instance of the comic method, using an anecdote which has been popular all over the world for twelve or fifteen hundred years. The teller tells it in this way: ...

As might be expected, Twain then goes on to provide an example of a story told in what he calls the "comic method." Thus, example is one technique he uses to develop his point. But it's certainly not the only one. Twain also divides stories into the categories of "humorous," "comic," and "witty." He defines each type of story, telling us that the humorous story is made humorous by *how* it is told, while the comic and witty stories derive their humor from *what* is told. And this sets Twain up to contrast the delivery of each type of story and to argue that because its point sneaks up on you, the humorous story is superior to the comic or witty. In contrasting the different types of stories, Twain ultimately analyzes the storytelling process—he teaches us "how to tell a story," as his title promises.

Not all essays rely on this many techniques to convey their point. In fact, some essayists develop their entire work largely around one main technique. So figure out which techniques will work best for your essay. Then start defining, describing, or dividing your subject to help readers see it as you do!

An illustration of Mark
Twain telling a story

Because essays are written to make a point, *what* you say in an essay is obviously critical. What some beginning essay writers overlook, however, is that *how* you say it is also important. Essays are not meant to be dry collections of facts; if you want anyone to read them, they should be written in a way that allows your voice to be heard and your style to be seen.

Before you decide on the style you will use for a specific essay, consider your audience. Who are you writing this piece for? Your teacher? Your friends or family? A local newspaper? Also think about your purpose in writing. Do you want to present research? Persuade readers to your way of thinking? Narrate a personal experience? Considering your audience and your purpose will help you to determine the most appropriate style for your essay. If you are writing a personal essay, for example, you will probably write in an informal, first person point of view (using "I"). A more formal essay or research paper, on the other hand, will likely be written in third person (using "he" or "she").

Even when you are writing in the third person,

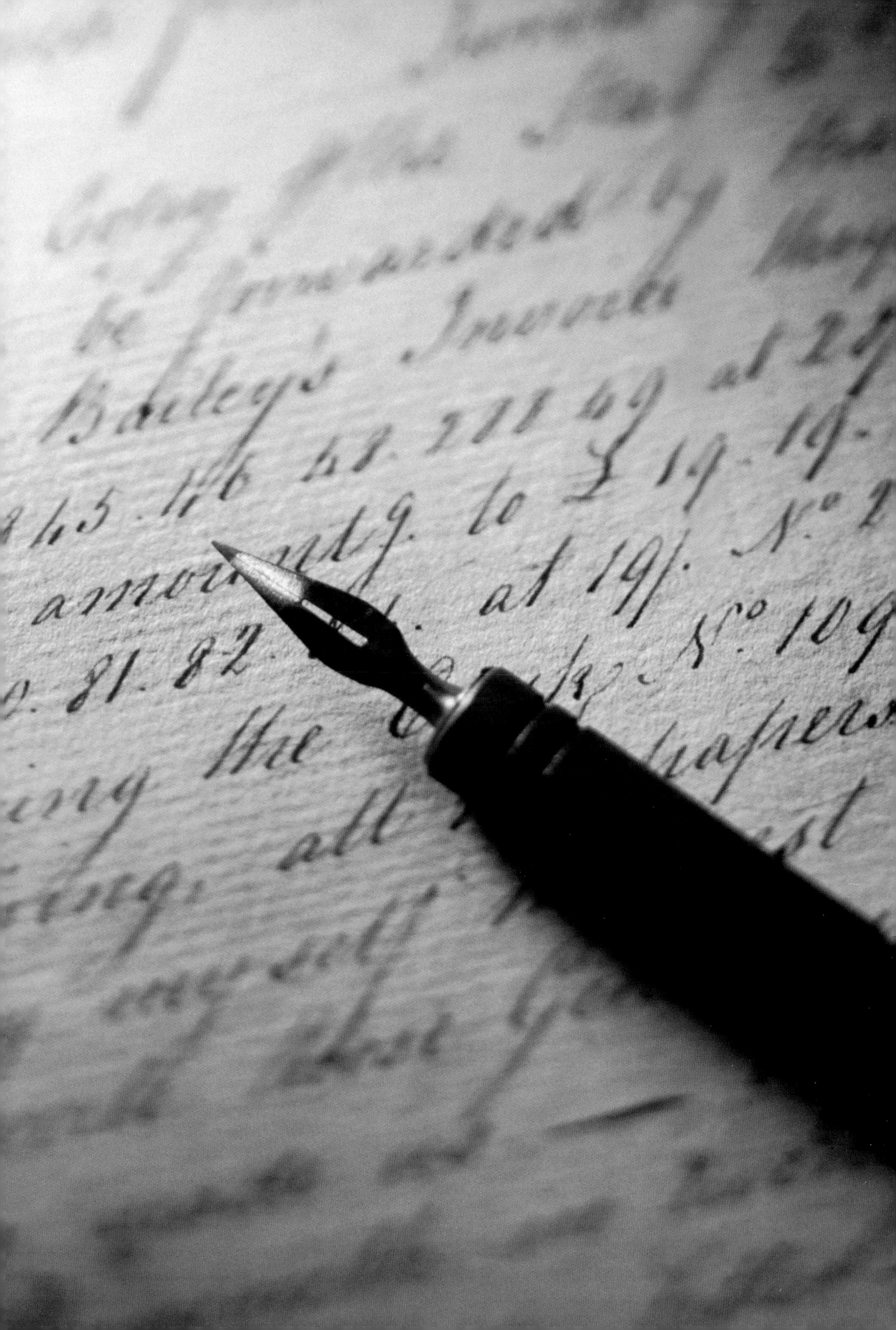

readers will likely still be able to sense something about you from the way in which you write, or your style. Maybe you use a lot of short, choppy sentences to convey a sense of urgency. Maybe you write long flowing `prose`, with sentences that meander here and there, in order to take readers into the depths of your thoughts. No matter your style, you should strive to be clear in your writing. Don't add fancy words simply to try to sound smart; making a clear, direct point is what will impress readers the most.

While your style can help to reveal something about you, the tone you adopt reveals your attitude toward your subject. It is important to match the tone of an essay to the subject; otherwise, readers won't be able to connect with your writing. For example, you might write about the death of a world leader in a solemn tone. An essay about your grandmother's apple pie, on the other hand, might employ a `reminiscent` tone (unless your grandmother never let you have any of the pie, in which case you might use an angry or complaining tone).

The following excerpt is taken from American
Indian writer Navarre Scott Momaday's essay "The
Way to Rainy Mountain" (1967). As you read, notice
the style and tone Momaday employs. What do they
say about him and his attitude toward his subject?

Writer N. Scott
Momaday (1934-)

A single knoll rises out of the plain in Oklahoma, north and west of the Wichita Range. For my people, the Kiowas, it is an old landmark, and they gave it the name Rainy Mountain. The hardest weather in the world is there. Winter brings blizzards, hot tornadic winds arise in the spring, and in summer the prairie is an anvil's edge.... At a distance in July or August the steaming foliage seems almost to writhe in fire....

I returned to Rainy Mountain in July. My grandmother had died in the spring, and I wanted to be at her grave....

When she was born, the Kiowas were living that last great moment of their history.... They never understood the grim, unrelenting advance of the U.S. Cavalry.... In order to save themselves, they surrendered to the soldiers at Fort Sill and were imprisoned in the old stone corral that now stands as a military museum. My grandmother was spared the humiliation of those high gray walls by eight or ten years, but she must have known from birth the affliction of defeat, the dark brooding of old warriors....

Now that I can have her only in memory, I see my grandmother in the several postures that were peculiar to her: standing at the wood stove on a winter morning and turning meat in a great iron skillet; sitting at the south window, bent above her beadwork,...; going out upon a cane, very slowly as she did when the weight of age came upon her; praying.... The last time I saw her she prayed standing by the side of her bed at night.... Transported so in the dancing light among the shadows of her room, she seemed beyond the reach of time. But that was illusion; I think I knew then that I should not see her again.

Based on the way he writes, how do you think Momaday feels about his grandmother's death? He grieves her loss, certainly, but his tone does not suggest despair. Instead, he looks back upon his grandmother's life and land in fond reminiscence. He wistfully recalls the glory days of the Kiowa, when his grandmother was born, before her people had surrendered to the U.S. government. Even as

A late-1800s Kiowa chief with bow and arrow

he recounts the Kiowa surrender, though, and the "affliction of defeat" that it brought upon the people, Momaday's tone does not become accusatory. He is not reproaching the U.S. government for destroying the ways of the Kiowa; rather, he is simply relating the history of his people.

Although Momaday writes in the first person, his style is not casual. While he reveals some very personal moments and insights, Momaday does not talk to us in the shorthand of one friend speaking to another. Instead, his long, flowing sentences give the essay a literary, almost lyrical, feel. With his careful uses of imagery, Momaday brings us into the land in which his people lived—a land that became an "anvil's edge" and seemed to "writhe in fire" during the summer. Such imagery draws us into the essay, allowing us to become completely absorbed in it.

When readers are absorbed in an essay, they can learn from it, grow from it, be changed by it. So the next time you are assigned an essay to write, don't groan. Instead, start thinking about all the great points you have to make. Then sit down with a pen or at a keyboard and start making them!

Getting Personal

Although you may think that nothing worth writing
about has ever happened to you, even the smallest
events in your life may strike a chord in readers,
allowing them to relate to or identify with you.
Think back to a time when you learned an important
lesson. Or think about someone who has played
an important role in your life or about a place
that has special meaning to you. Write a personal
essay about that experience, person, or place.
But don't just write an anecdote. Make a point.
Perhaps helping your dad build a birdhouse, for
example, led you to realize that parents aren't
perfect. After you've written your essay, show
it to your family or friends. Ask them what they
think the point of the essay is. If they aren't
sure, go back and revise, or change, your writing
to make your point clearer.

Thinking in Specifics

Although essays can be written about anything and everything, choosing a topic specific enough to be the focus of an essay can take some work. First, think of something that interests you. Since most of us have fairly broad interests, chances are your idea will not be quite specific enough to write an essay about. In order to make your topic more manageable, make a list of all the things that come to mind when you think of it. Are any of these specific enough to form the basis of an essay? If not, try to narrow your idea even further. For example, perhaps your train of thought runs something like this: plants—insects that rely on plants—butterflies—plants that butterflies prefer—creating a butterfly garden. After you've narrowed your topic, head to the library and make a list of potential sources. If there aren't any, you may need to pick a different subject.

Building a Strong Structure

No matter how beautiful a house is, it will fall
flat if it's not built on a strong structure.
The same is true of essays. Practice organizing your writing by constructing an essay about
an abstract idea such as love, hate, patriotism,
or beauty. Everyone has their own opinions about
these subjects, so you must make your reader see
yours. Begin with an introduction that grabs readers' interest. Be sure that your introduction also
includes your thesis, or the point you will prove.
Use the body of your essay to support the thesis.
You might offer examples of people who have demonstrated patriotism, for example. Or you might
narrate a story about hate. Maybe you will divide
and classify different types of love or compare
something you think is beautiful with something
that is not. Bring your essay to a compelling conclusion, one that leaves us feeling that you have
made your point and the essay is complete.

Seeing the Style

One of the best ways to learn how to write anything is to read. Go back and reread the essays
excerpted in this book. Decide which you like
best. Now think about how the essay would have been
different if it had been written in another tone
or style. For example, what if Joseph Addison had
written his essay about ladies' headdresses in an
angry, judgmental tone? Or what if Mark Twain had
written his essay in a "literary," ornate style?
Don't just imagine it, write it! For example, you
might change Twain's plainspoken, "The humorous
story is told gravely" to "The humorous chronicle
is related in all solemnity and somberness." When
you are finished, analyze the result. What do you
think the author achieved by writing in the tone or
style he chose to adopt, rather than in yours?

LOSSARY

abstract a quality, emotion, or idea that cannot be defined by the senses

cite to acknowledge as the source of a quotation or fact; in a research paper, sources are usually cited within the text or in a footnote

dialogues works of literature that are written as if they were a conversation between two people

explicitly obviously; an explicit thesis is written out in full, and its meaning is specific

fiction literary works in which situations, characters, and events are made up; novels and short stories are works of fiction

first person a perspective, pronoun, or verb form that refers to the speaker or writer; in English, "I" and "we" are first-person pronouns

narration the telling of a story, as opposed to exposition (which generally provides background information)

nonfiction writing that is based on facts rather than fiction

primary sources sources that provide firsthand information; primary sources include interviews with subjects, autobiographies and diaries written by subjects, and letters

prose speech or writing that is not poetry but sounds more like everyday speech

reminiscent describing the act of looking back on the past, often in a fond way

secondary sources sources that provide information about a subject based on an analysis or interpretation of primary sources; secondary sources include books and newspaper articles written about the subject

third person a perspective, pronoun, or verb form that refers to someone or something being spoken about; in English, third-person pronouns include "he," "she," "it," and "they"

tragic hero a literary character who either has a flaw or makes a mistake in judgment that leads to a tragic outcome

Victorian Age the time period, from 1837 to 1901, during which Queen Victoria reigned in England; attitudes at the time were generally stiff and conventional

SELECTED Ⓑ IBLIOGRAPHY

Brown, Sharon, ed. *Essays of our Times*. Chicago: Scott, Foresman and Company, 1928.

Gross, John, ed. *The Oxford Book of Essays*. New York: Oxford University Press, 1991.

Lopate, Phillip, comp. *The Art of the Personal Essay: An Anthology from the Classical Era to the Present*. New York: Doubleday, 1994.

McCuen, Jo Ray, and Anthony C. Winkler. *Readings for Writers*. New York: Harcourt College Publishers, 2001.

Oates, Joyce Carol, and Robert Atwan, eds. *The Best American Essays of the Century*. Boston: Houghton Mifflin Company, 2000.

Turabian, Kate. *A Manual for Writers of Research Papers, Theses, and Dissertations*. Chicago: University of Chicago Press, 2007.

Zinsser, William. *On Writing Well: The Classic Guide to Writing Nonfiction*. New York: HarperCollins, 1994.

❶NDEX